THE TRANQUIL SERIES II

VIGNESHWARAN GANAPATHI

Copyright © Vigneshwaran Ganapathi
All Rights Reserved.

To all those who hope for Peace and Liberty, Education Institutions, Policy Makers, Future Policy Makers, Educationalists, Students, and Commons

Contents

Preface

Creating the cave of policy-making is a generational process, Before and after "The Tranquil Series II" suggestions and ideas are made by many Law and Policy Makers. As a common, in today's world, we contribute together to choose our representative and Head of the Government. The Policymakers of any nation should understand people and their intention in creating policy. Kindling each and everyone for their contribution to policy-making this book is penned. I have bundled the blog "Tranquility wins" incidents and baselined the matters we should be conscious of making policies. Irrespective of our profession we may come up with a question "Is it something for me?" Yes, The concept of democracy is to turn King is the Law into Law is the King, and the law and policies are made by the commons through a representative. Even we may do it in our future days. I hope this book can give a drastic thought process and the idea of policy-making in each incident.

> *"The Power of the Head of Government is from a contribution of commoners"*
>
> -Vigneshwaran Ganapathi

Acknowledgements

An empty paper before you is more valuable than the written one, A vision of making something productive is required when making empty paper valuable. Thanking each word that makes me run for that great vision;

I Thank,

Mii "Celebrating May 1"

My Family, & "We 4 the 404",

All my brothers and sisters,

Bloggers and writers made me find incidents in various books and blogs.

I want to thank EVERYONE who ever said anything positive to me or taught me something. I heard it all, and it meant something.

I want to thank God "Someone, Who is the creator of me" most of all because without God I wouldn't be able to do any of this.

For Policy Makers

I find many reasons to bind my blogs as a book but one main reason is to draft some incidents which can suggest to us some policy-making ideas

CHAPTER ONE

The Future Makers

We are in 2022, We have the right to speak and express ourselves. We have the right to vote and contribute to democracy. But take a year in B.C the rulers invade other countries and rule the country. The Empire's ups and down and succession were determined through royal family rules. Dynasties history cleared us commons are not to be part as head of the governments. In today's world, you have an option to become a Prime Minister / Minister / President / Head of the Government, etc. How did this great concept of making commons to represent the Country's Government evolve? We have different questions on this. But this is not the book ok states Democracy but to understand the action of democracy by making the right policy for the people via people representation.

> *"A right policy can be made only when the House of Commons filled with right commoners"*

Today you may sit on your working desk or class desk or may lie on your bed reading this, But tomorrow you may be in place to create policy for the country and people. You may be into action policymaking. This book is a bundle of my blog writing and described version of it. My survey and search of various reading and surfing times made me undergo this writing work on understanding things that when a policymaker should understand before creating it. We have policymakers millions today, We have many houses of commons all around the world representing people but the question on people policy remains rest to us to find loops. This book is also for the policymakers to correct the error if any, and also for the future coming policymakers.

The term "Policy" mentioned in the coming pages is referred as National policies made by the policy makers for the country.

Tranquility Wins

CHAPTER TWO

The Great Famine of Ukraine

"

It was an evening I started surfing about Ukraine and Russian conflict, And I wished to read about the history of Ukraine. I come across the word "Holodomor" in a paragraph that stopped me to read the back history and Kindled me to start exploring it. The statement "Holodomor, A man-made famine that convulsed the Soviet republic of Ukraine from 1932 to 1933, peaking in the late spring of 1933." And It questioned, Is the first time people of Ukraine face a crisis?

Why Ukraine? Why such Man-made Famine? What is the Soviet reason behind it?

Joseph Stalin and Breadbasket

Joseph Vissarionovich Stalin was a Georgian revolutionary and Soviet political leader who governed the Soviet Union from 1922 until his death in 1953. Stalin wanted the country, with its hugely fertile black soil, to be the breadbasket of the Soviet Union. He wanted to feed the important party officials and export its grain abroad to fund his vast industrialization projects. It was an unmitigated disaster. Farmers were no longer paid for their produce but worked according to a ration system based on their productivity. In reality, it made them beholden to the party, which, controlling their finances, was able to control all aspects of their lives. And they were no longer able to buy food.

The Man-Made Famine In the 1930s, Soviet leaders under Joseph Stalin engineered a famine that killed millions as they sought to consolidate agricultural power. In Ukraine, they used additional force as they sought to clamp down on a burgeoning Ukrainian national identity. So many Ukrainians died that officials had to send people to resettle the area, setting off a demographic shift. As hunger spread among residents, Stalin spearheaded a disinformation campaign to hide the truth from other Soviet citizens and the world. At least 5 million people died from starvation in the Soviet Union between 1931 and 1934 including 3.9 million Ukrainians.

Holodomor

Holodomor Between 1917 and 1921, Ukraine briefly became an independent country and fought to retain its independence before succumbing to the Red Army and being incorporated into the Soviet Union. In the 1920s, Soviet central authorities, seeking the support of the populace, allowed for some cultural autonomy through the policy known as "indigenization." By the end of the 1920s, Soviet leader Joseph Stalin decided to curtail Ukraine's cultural autonomy, launching the intimidation, arrest, imprisonment, and execution of thousands of Ukrainian intellectuals, church leaders, as well as Communist Party functionaries who had supported Ukraine's distinctiveness. The majority of Ukrainians, who were small-scale or subsistence farmers, resisted. The state confiscated the property of the independent farmers and forced them to work on government collective farms. This created a Man-made famine in the region, referred to as the great famine "Holodomor". Ukraine, with its history of resistance to Soviet rule, was a threat to the Soviet regime. Fearing that opposition to his policies in Ukraine could intensify and possibly lead to Ukraine's secession from the Soviet Union, Stalin set unrealistically high grain procurement quotas. Those quotas were accompanied by other Draconian measures intended to wipe out a significant part of the Ukrainian nation.

In August of 1932, the decree of "Five Stalks of Grain," stated that anyone, even a child, caught taking any product from a collective field, could be shot or imprisoned for stealing "socialist property." At the beginning of 1933, about 54,645 people were tried and sentenced; of those, 2,000 were executed. As famine escalated, growing numbers of farmers left their villages in search of food outside of Ukraine. Directives sent by Stalin and Molotov

(Stalin's closest collaborator) in January of 1933 prevented them from leaving, effectively sealing the borders of Ukraine. To further ensure that Ukrainian farmers did not leave their villages to seek food in the cities, the Soviet government started a system of internal passports, which were denied to farmers so they could not travel or obtain a train ticket without official permission. These same restrictions applied to the Kuban region of Russia, which borders Ukraine, and in which Ukrainians made up the largest portion of the Kuban population - 67 percent. At the time of the Holodomor, over one-third of the villages in Ukraine were put on "blacklists" for failing to meet grain quotas. Blacklisted villages were encircled by troops and residents were blockaded from leaving or receiving any supplies; it was essentially a collective death sentence.

To ensure these new laws were strictly enforced, groups of "activists" organized by the Communist Party were dispatched to the countryside. As described by historian Clarence Manning: "The work of these special 'commissions' and 'brigades' was marked by the utmost severity. They entered the villages and made the most thorough searches of the houses and barns of every peasant. They dug up the earth and broke into the walls of buildings and stoves in which the peasants tried to hide their last handfuls of food."

To escape death by starvation, people in the villages ate anything that was edible: grass, acorns, even cats and dogs. Contemporary Soviet police archives contain descriptions of the immense suffering and despair of Ukrainian farmers, including instances of lawlessness, theft, lynching, and even cannibalism. This Famine, the Holodomor, resulted in widespread deaths and mass graves dug across the countryside. The official registers did not give a full accounting of what was happening across Ukraine - deaths often remained unregistered, cause of death was missing - to conceal the true situation.

At the height of the Holodomor in June of 1933, Ukrainians were dying at a rate of 28,000 people per day. Around 3.9 million Ukrainians died during the Holodomor of 1932-33 (as established in a 2015 study by a team of demographers from the Ukrainian Institute of Demographic and Social Studies, and the University of North Carolina-Chapel Hill). While Ukrainians were dying, the Soviet state extracted 4.27 million tons of grain from Ukraine in 1932, enough to feed at least 12 million people for an entire year. Soviet records show that in January of 1933, there were enough grain reserves in the USSR to feed well over 10 million people. The government could have organized famine relief and could have accepted help from outside of the USSR. Moscow rejected foreign aid and denounced those who offered it, instead of exporting Ukraine's grain and other foodstuffs abroad for cash.

Most historians, who have studied this period in Ukrainian history, have concluded that the Famine was deliberate and linked to a broader Soviet policy to subjugate the Ukrainian people. With the fall of the Soviet Union and the opening of Soviet government archives (including archives of the security services), researchers have been able to demonstrate that Soviet authorities undertook measures specifically in Ukraine with the knowledge that the result would be the deaths of millions of Ukrainians by starvation. "The Terror-Famine of 1932-33 was a dual-purpose by-product of collectivization, designed to suppress Ukrainian nationalism and the most important concentration of prosperous peasants at one throw." –Norman Davies, Europe, A History.

The Russian Denial

The USSR vigorously denied that the Holodomor had occurred. Since the collapse of the Soviet Union, the Communist Party, secret police, and government archives that have become accessible to researchers support the conclusion that the famine was caused by Soviet state policies and was indeed intentionally intensified by Soviet authorities.

Raphael Lemkin and Soviet Genocide

Raphael Lemkin (1900-1959), an expert in international criminal law (with a particular interest in the prevention of mass human extermination), who coined and promoted the term "genocide," identified the Holodomor as "the classic example of Soviet genocide." Lemkin's ideas on genocide served as the basis of the United Nations Convention on the Prevention and Punishment of Genocide in 1948. The Convention defines genocide as acts "having the intent to destroy, in whole or in part, a national, ethnic, racial or religious group, as such."

In a speech given in 1953, as well as in articles written in the 1950s, Lemkin applied the term genocide to the Holodomor and the attempt to destroy the Ukrainian nation.

Lemkin identified four integral components in the genocidal process in Ukraine:

- The decimation of the Ukrainian national elites (political and cultural leaders),
- The destruction of the Ukrainian Autocephalous (independent) Orthodox Church (its clergy and hierarchy),
- The starvation of the Ukrainian farming population (the Holodomor), and
- Its replacement with non-Ukrainians from the RSFSR and elsewhere.

Leading historians and other scholars, such as James Mace, Robert Conquest, Timothy Snyder, Norman Naimark, Anne Applebaum, who has devoted significant time to studying the Holodomor and have published extensively on the subject have all concluded that it was genocide

Peace Ahead

Tranquility wins - Vladimir Putin shattered the peace in Europe by unleashing a war on the democracy of 44 million people, his justification was that modern, Western-leaning Ukraine was a constant threat and Russia could not feel "safe, develop and exist". But after thousands of deaths in ruined towns and cities and the displacement of more than 10 million people inside Ukraine and beyond. One in common is, They are on the same floor of control, and couldn't choose independently to be democratic from the 1920s. Peace wins negative as a craving in people's minds somewhere they could find it and bring up their children in a tranquil world. It may lead to another debate on who is on the right stand but the left things were people's dreams and projection of life."

Creating the right policy is very important, Finding it right is in hands of makers, increasing the human development index. Glitches in making the right policy can create a dark history

1) Create a Right Policy

CHAPTER THREE

Collapsed Lira

We were recently aware of Srilankan economic crisis, On reading articles regarding a view on the other side of the impact when policy doesn't stick with country growth we get the wrong sidestepped not the remedies to solve, Not with Srilanka the incident is with Turkey. Turkey has been dealing with the currency and debt crisis for a long time. The value of the Turkish Lira USD/TRY has been in a free fall losing significant value against the dollar. Turkey's economy is likely to expand at a much slower pace this year as rising domestic macro-economic and financial challenges moderate growth in 2022 following an unexpectedly strong economic growth in 2021, says the latest edition of the World Bank's Turkey Economic Monitor report.

Why Turkey? Why such a fall? What is the reason behind this Economic Crisis?

The Policy

The simple reason for the Turkish lira's collapse is the unorthodox economic policy of keeping interest rates low to boost Turkey's economic growth and export potential with a competitive currency. For many economists, if inflation goes up you control it by raising interest rates. But Mr. Erdogan sees interest rates as "an evil that make the rich richer and the poor poorer".

The Inflation Rate

Annual inflation has surged above 21% in Turkey, but the Central Bank of the Republic of Turkey, overhauled by Mr. Erdogan, has just lowered interest rates from 16% to 15%, the third cut this year. Inflation is rising around the world, and central banks are talking about hiking interest rates. But not here, because Mr. Erdogan believes ultimately inflation will fall. Turkey's economy is heavily dependent upon imports for producing goods from foods to textiles, so the rise of the dollar against the lira has a direct impact on the price of consumer products.

The Turkish lira has lost roughly 47% of its value in the last full year, in a rout driven by Erdogan's refusal to raise rates as inflation consistently climbed. The currency's turbulence has hit Turks hard, as the value of their salaries dropped and living costs dramatically increased. Steep hikes in electricity and natural gas tariffs have compounded the pain for consumers and businesses. The government has instead promoted "permanent liraisation," and a "rescue plan" that would see the Turkish central bank guarantee savings in lira by stepping in and making up losses to lira deposits if their value against hard currencies falls beyond the interest rates set by banks. Analysts say the plan is costly and is essentially a largely hidden interest rate hike, and not likely to be sustainable in the longer term. "Inflation will stay close to these high levels until the very final months of this year, but the central bank and, crucially, President Erdogan seems to have no appetite for interest rate hikes,"

Vulnerable Position

With the Turkish lira slumping to record lows and the country experiencing skyrocketing inflation, Turkey's economy is quickly accelerating downwards. This presents a risk for the country's President, Recep Tayyip Erdogan, whose popularity has been on the decline. Ahead of upcoming elections in 2023, the combination of a collapsing economy and the government's plummeting support has put Erdogan in an extremely vulnerable position.

Lira Collapse

Erdogan has stuck fast to his policies, opposing interest rate hikes -- which he calls "the mother and father of all evil" High-interest rates are a drag on activity and slow down economic growth, but they are useful to tamp down inflation as they cut demand and encourage savings. The

COVID-19 pandemic added to the problem, and negatively impacted poverty reduction. While pandemic-related fiscal support measures helped soften the blow, it is estimated that the pandemic pushed an additional 1.6 million people below the $5.50 poverty line in 2020, raising Turkey's poverty rate to 12.2 percent, from 10.2 percent in 2019. It is also estimated that a 1 percent increase in consumer prices in Turkey raises the number of poor by 2 percent, although income support and changes to consumption patterns could dampen this effect. With official statistics showing annual inflation has increased from 15 percent in January 2021 to 48.7 percent in January 2022, it is likely that the poverty rate remained high in 2021.

Future Plans

Growth is set to decline to 2 percent this year, from an estimated 10 percent in 2021, firming to a modest 3 percent in 2023, as high inflation and policy uncertainty weigh on private consumption and investment. As in 2021, growth in 2022 is expected to be largely driven by robust growth in exports to the European Union (EU), with the additional prospect of growth in tourism. Recent macro-financial instability has put pressure on bank balance sheets and undermined efforts to develop domestic sources of long-term finance. Risks to the outlook are tilted to the downside. The headwinds include risks from the pandemic at home and abroad, climate change-related disasters, price pressures and value chain disruptions at the level of the global economy, and the prospect of interest rate tightening in advanced economies and the resulting tightening of global liquidity conditions. "Mitigating the risks to the growth outlook of 2022 and 2023 will require well-coordinated monetary and fiscal policies that stabilize the economy in the short term and allow attention to be reoriented towards realizing Turkey's growth potential in the medium term," said Hans Beck, World Bank's Lead Country Economist for Turkey.

The Impact of War

The war in Ukraine couldn't have come at a worse time for the Turkish economy. Amid the country's ongoing economic crisis, the government has been implementing extraordinary and unconventional monetary and fiscal policies. The aim is to ensure a steady, but ultimately unsustainable, foreign trade surplus by taking advantage of the undervalued local currency. Its approach has two main components. First, the Central Bank of the Republic of Turkey is implementing too low of a policy interest rate (14%) compared to the real (54.4%) and expected (26.4%) levels of inflation. Second, state-owned banks are ramping up lending, resulting in strong credit growth.

To offset the significant side effects, which are persistently high inflation and greater fragility of the financial stability, other measures are being taken, including covertly selling foreign exchange (FX) reserves via state-owned banks and directing local investors to the newly introduced FX-protected deposit program. The super-shock of the currency crisis last November and December, when the exchange rate of the Turkish lira shot from 9.60 to the dollar to 18.40, could be alleviated by these tools. However, inflationary expectations also shifted dramatically upward, resulting in a boom in pent-up household consumption. Going forward, businesses are hesitant about making new investments as economic instability and volatility worsen. Foreign investors already lost their confidence in Turkish lira-denominated financial assets in early 2021 and their appetite for hard currency ones was also killed in late 2021.

The Russian invasion of Ukraine triggered the imposition of harsh sanctions on Moscow by the European Union, Britain, Canada, and the United States. Turkey has not joined any of these sanctions. Energy costs in Turkey began to rise, but, as with the price of wheat, Russia's invasion of Ukraine has sent them soaring. Turkey imports about a third of its gas from Russia. The state-owned pipeline operator Botas said this month that the price of gas for electricity generation would rise by almost 45%, with a 50% rise in prices for industry and 35% for households.

Peace Ahead

Witnessing the above we can observe the political view which is not enough to understand the pain of people on the projection of their life. they suffer from inflation, they suffer to plan new for next-generation, It creates a hurdle to dream. When a framework fails, it hits but when a policy fails, it kills. A right and a progressive policy are very important when it comes to national interest irrespective of any country, and it is highly prioritized when it is economic related item. The people's new dream is the government's highest progress.

Changes in the policy should be futuristic, only then it can find the way to sustainable development. Same when it comes to Finance, A economic policy should be futuristic and progressive, only then it can make the coming days safe.

2) Create a policy futuristic and progressive

•

CHAPTER FOUR

Decades of Socialism

In search of Che Guevara on surfing, I come up with a statement "Three main ideological positions are behind the debate over current changes in Cuba: the statist position, which seeks to perfect a top-down, state socialism; the economist position, which defends market socialism; and the self-management position, which favors democratic socialism and worker participation in company decision making."

Why Cuba? Why Socialism? Why such a turn?

Independence

Cuba first started to fight for its independence from Spain in 1868 in the Ten Years War. Led by national hero Jose Marti, the war for independence again became heated in 1895. In 1898 the United States became involved in the war when one of its battleships, the USS Maine, was sunk. The US gained control of Cuba with the Treaty of Paris and, in 1902, gave Cuba independence.

The Dictator Vs Fidel

In 1952, a former president of Cuba named Fulgencio Batista took control of the country and made himself dictator. Many of the people of Cuba were not happy with this. Rebel leader Fidel Castro organized a revolution to overthrow Batista. In 1959, Fidel Castro was able to overthrow Batista's government and gain control of the country. He declared Cuba a socialist country and allied Cuba with the Soviet Union. His legacy in Cuba and elsewhere has been a mixed record of social progress and abject poverty, racial equality, political persecution, medical advances, and a degree of misery comparable to the conditions that existed in Cuba when he entered Havana as a victorious guerrilla commander in 1959.

The Turn

Cuba became a major player in the Cold War between the United States and the Soviet Union. First, the United States unsuccessfully tried to overthrow Castro through the Bay of Pigs invasion. Then, the Soviet Union tried to establish a nuclear missile base in Cuba causing the Cuban Missile Crisis. Fidel Castro remained in power for 50 years and then handed over the government to his younger brother

Raul. There is no doubt that the Castro era created a generous social welfare program – free healthcare, education, and social security system that has been a cornerstone of the Cuban economy for the last six decades. But there is still no denying that after the collapse of the Soviet Union, which was the biggest benefactor of the communist revolution in Cuba, the Cuban economy has been in a tight squeeze, especially with the US-led embargo in operation for decades. President Barack Obama initiated moves to normalize relations with Cuba and to lift the embargo in 2014, but President Donald Trump has all but reversed that process. The Cuban economy badly needs to embark upon an alternative course if the task of the state is to go beyond fulfilling the basic needs of the people. Many Cubans are fleeing the nation because they find the environment both politically and economically strangulating. Only 11 million Cubans remain on the island today. Fidel Castro was an orthodox communist who could not bring himself around to the idea of adopting market economy reforms. His brother Raul Castro, when he replaced Fidel in the high office, took baby steps to usher in a certain degree of privatization he allowed Cubans to buy and sell residences; he relaxed rules to help Cubans become self-employed entrepreneurs, but he backtracked when the new businessmen made a clamor for structural reforms to successfully pursue the economic activity. There was a backlash from within the communist party bigwigs who felt that the economic concessions would threaten the communist stranglehold.

Socialism

Cuba's experience of socialism has its specific characteristics, which we must situate historically to properly understand their implications. The Cuban Revolution and its aftermath can help us think about the relationship between socialism and democracy and how that relationship is reflected in Cuba's contemporary political difficulties and the possibilities for new left-wing politics on the island and in the larger region. The New President is, like his predecessors, quite steeped in economic and political orthodoxy. He is neither a votary of economic liberalization nor of political freedom. That is why possibly he was chosen that he would uphold, not deviate from, the 'revolutionary line'. To appreciate the impact of the Cuban socialist experience on the thinking of the region's left, we need a historical analysis. The influence of the Cuban Revolution was very different from the 1960s to the 1980s, in the heat of guerrilla movements and Latin-American dictatorships, then it was in the 1990s, after the collapse of the communist bloc. It was different at the beginning of the 2000s, at the onset of Latin America's "Pink Tide," than it is today. Neither in Cuba nor the region as a whole can the politics and ideas of the left be treated as monoliths. For at least two decades now, however, the left in Cuba has been growing more diverse, even while the bastions of official power do not necessarily offer it openings, and even though the anti-government opposition politics associated with the U.S. government has not changed.

The pluralism of the leftist political field in Cuba draws its power from a different base: Cuban civil society. Projects, collectives, and organizations have sprung up around a variety of issues: environmentalism, feminism, anti-racism, animal rights, artistic freedoms, and so on. These groups have pushed forward the democratization of public space, institutional policies that expand rights, and the legal-organizational capacity of social actors. In that way, Cuban civil society is becoming more and more similar to many others around the world.

The shift

The constituent process for the constitution took place after the exit of Raúl Castro, who had succeeded Fidel Castro as the president of Cuba in 2006. The shift in political leadership under new president Miguel Díaz-

Canel, the changes in the country, and a crisis of the left across Latin America, signal new possibilities for Cuba. But it may lead to violating the history of making Cuba and its socialism. Irrespective of the violation a policy on balancing both the Market economy and socialism deriving something new may come up to understand Cuba later.

The shift in a policy can be made only when the conservative areas are derived, If not, it can make us violate our policies later.

3) A healthy shift in policy should create a wealthy economy

CHAPTER FIVE

The White Gold Politics

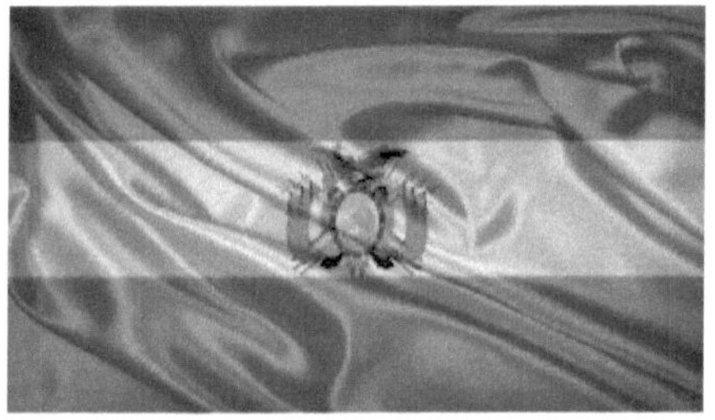

The overthrow of Bolivian president Evo Morales shows how the politics of environmentalism and social justice intersect in a silvery-white metal. Since 2019, Bolivia has been in a state of political turmoil. Accusations of election fraud during the presidential election that year led to the resignation of longtime President Evo Morales. This event motivated many Bolivians, including supporters of the Morales' party, the left-wing Movement for Socialism (MAS), to demand more transparency from both government institutions and political parties.

What White Metal? Why Politics of Environmentalism? Why Bolivia?

The Large Deposit

Lithium batteries are the most energetic ever created and have inspired hopes that electric vehicles can help reverse climate change, as well as expectations of a boom in "white petroleum" or "white gold," as boosters refer to lithium. Its goal with lithium was to produce raw materials and battery components as part of a plan to foster domestic industrialization. Bolivia has at least a quarter of the world's lithium, including the single largest deposit in the Salar de Uyuni, a salt pan so large it can be seen from space.

Bolivian political crisis

South America's second-poorest country, Bolivia, is home to one of the world's richest reserves of lithium, a key component in batteries that power everything from electric cars to remote controls. On a continent where the exploitation of natural resources has enriched multinational corporations and corrupt governments — but scarcely any of the people who live there — lithium's potential to spark an economic renaissance in Bolivia has not inspired optimism. Until now.

Since his election in 2020, President Luis Arce, an economist by training, has spearheaded a massive nationalization of lithium's supply chain. The goal is to meet 40 percent of the world's lithium demand by 2030, making Bolivia the "world capital of lithium," in his words.

Bolivia is home to the world's largest lithium resources. Together with Chile and Argentina, the so-called "lithium triangle" holds almost 60 percent of the planet's known lithium deposits, according to the U.S. Geological Survey. But while Chile and Argentina are among the top global producers, alongside Australia and China, Bolivia has yet to produce lithium in commercial quantities. For two decades, successive governments have tried to jump-start Bolivia's lithium industry, attempting both pro-market and statist strategies, with unimpressive results. Efforts at privatizing the industry in the 1990s failed. So did attempts by longtime President Evo Morales to expand the government's role in the industry through a state-owned lithium company and to promote local production of batteries and electric vehicles.

The 2019 Bolivian political crisis occurred on 10 November 2019, after 21 days of civil protests following the disputed 2019 Bolivian general election. The elections took place after a referendum to amend the Bolivian constitution, which limits the number of terms to two, was rejected in 2016, but the Supreme Court of Justice ruled that all public offices would have no term limits despite what was established in the constitution and allowing Morales to run for a fourth term.

The Political Turn

Lithium-rich Bolivia has been thrown into political turmoil after its longstanding president, socialist Evo Morales, was exiled to Argentina amid vote-rigging accusations. Due to the expected exponential growth in demand for battery technology in recent years, of which lithium is a component, interest in Bolivia's untapped reserves has skyrocketed. However, unlike neighboring countries Argentina and Chile, which both have lithium mines in production, efforts to develop these resources have so far amounted to little.

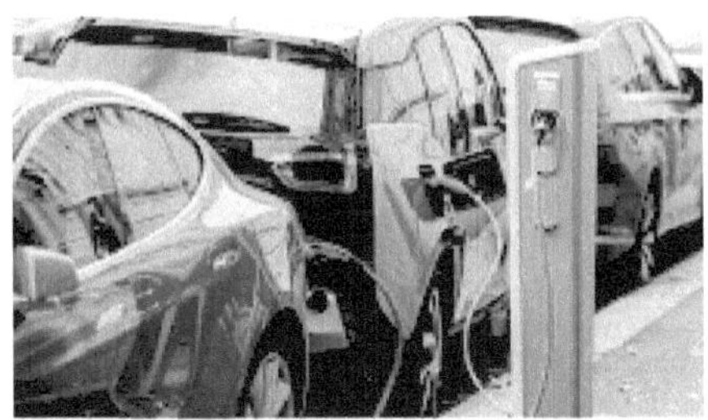

The Russian invasion has come just as Ukraine, under President Volodymyr Zelenskyy, was trying to position itself as a major player in the clean energy transition — an evolution for a country that long built its economy on coal, iron, titanium, and other legacy industries. Ukraine started to auction off exploration permits to develop its lithium reserves, as well as copper, cobalt, and nickel. All are natural resources that play critical roles in the clean energy technology essential to the shift away from fossil fuels that scientists say is necessary to ward off the worst consequences of climate change. The move holds a "strategic importance for the establishment of Ukraine on the global stage, in a new role," Roman Opimakh, head of the State Geological Service of Ukraine, said in May at a flagship presentation for global investors. Ukraine's potential for lithium production had started to attract global attention. In November, European Lithium, an Australian firm, said it was in the process of securing rights to two promising lithium deposits in the Donetsk region, in eastern Ukraine, and Kirovograd, in the center of the country. The company said at the time it aimed to become

Europe's largest lithium supplier. While lithium isn't a particularly rare resource, it is currently virtually irreplaceable in batteries, and demand is expected to skyrocket as electric vehicles take off, sending automakers scrambling to secure enough supply. Lithium prices have risen by as much as 600% over 2021. And there are growing concerns that the world's supply of lithium, as well as other minerals critical to the clean energy transition, are controlled by a handful of countries. China, Congo, and Australia account for three-fourths of the global output of lithium, cobalt, and rare earths.

The Deals

Bolivia's abundant lithium reserves are mostly located within the country's spectacular salt flats, called the Salar de Uyuni. The area, which is popular with tourists, is home to the largest salt flats in the world. There were plans agreed by a privately-owned German firm called ACI Systems Alemania (ACISA) and Bolivia's state-owned lithium company, YLB, to develop a lithium mine in the region. However, these had resulted in widespread protests as locals said the agreement to build a mine, an electric vehicle battery factory, and a lithium hydroxide plant did not deliver enough local benefits. Eventually, the project was shelved. At the time, Morales said the government had gone with China over the others because the country has the world's biggest demand for lithium.

The Tranquility Wins Link

The reason for the overthrown and economic move for lithium links with each other due to the socialistic move of the government in deal with allies turned to take a step for corporates for the lithium need for future manufacture of batteries. The coming years can be high in the hands of electric mobility and the green side of transportation which vitally depends on lithium. This is the reason why a great political and economical finger was pointed at the country Bolivia. There is a huge difference between having mineral resources in the ground and turning those into economically viable mineral reserves. "Resources" refers to minerals in the ground; "reserves" are resources that can be mined or otherwise extracted at a reasonable cost. That means only a fraction of a country's resources can ever be considered economically viable reserves, let alone commercially competitive. But the delay in the policy making can resist a countries development what this incident project us.

The Delay on good policy is not good when it ignores the economic stimulation, Making a country politically strong and increasing the productivity of making policy is very important when it can stimulate the economy and grow up the country

4) A delay in making the right policy can ignore the economic stimulation

The Grisly End

This incident is a little back from the past ones. The last minutes in Gaddafi's life have gained a grisly status, A spectacle of pain and humiliation, the end of the man who once styled himself the "king of the kings of Africa" has been told in snatches of mobile phone footage and blurry stills and contradictory statements.

Why Gaddafi? Why Libya? Why such Death?

Muammar Gaddafi

He was a Libyan revolutionary, politician, and political theorist. He governed Libya as Revolutionary Chairman of the Libyan Arab Republic from 1969 to 1977 and then as the "Brotherly Leader" of the Great Socialist People's Libyan Arab Jamahiriya from 1977 to 2011. He was initially ideologically committed to Arab nationalism and Arab socialism but later ruled according to his own Third International Theory. In 1973, Gaddafi finally began outlining the ideology of the new Libyan Arab Republic. On the 15th of April at Zwara, Gaddafi outlined 'the five points for the continuation of the revolution. Firstly, to 'abrogate all laws', with the intent that new laws be developed as they're needed. Gaddafi does explain that these are only state laws, while Islamic law still holds people to account. Secondly, to purge the country of counter-revolutionaries. Thirdly, 'freedom for the people, announcing a desire to aid the majority of people and even to hand out guns to an allied civilian militia and revolutionize the whole populace. Fourthly, the destruction of bureaucracy, and fifthly, a desired 'cultural revolution'.

For Libya

From 1974 onward Gaddafi espoused a form of Islamic socialism as expressed in The Green Book. His government financed a broad spectrum of revolutionary or terrorist groups worldwide, including the Black Panthers and the Nation of Islam in the United States and the Irish Republican Army in Northern Ireland. Libya's purported involvement in the destruction of a civilian airliner in 1988 over Lockerbie, Scotland, led to United Nations (UN) and U.S. sanctions that further isolated Gaddafi from the international community. After letting the Green Book simmer in the background for two years, the break with Egypt gave Gaddafi the excuse to go all in. On March 2nd, 1977, Gaddafi adopted the 'Declaration on the

Establishment of the Authority of the People'. Starting by reiterating loyalty to both 'socialism' and Islam, a list of new changes was outlined, beginning with the renaming of the country. Libya under Gaddafi was now known as the Socialist People's Libyan Arab Jamahiriya. Jamahiriya is broadly defined to mean 'state of the masses' and can be considered a kind of people's republic. Particularly notable was the statement that the 'authority of the people would now be enacted through People's Congresses

The African Union

In February 2009 Gaddafi was elected chairman of the African Union (AU), and later that year he gave his first speech before the UN General Assembly. The lengthy critical speech, in which he threw a copy of the UN charter, generated a significant measure of controversy within the international community.

New Interest

Gaddafi fitted the bill as an authoritarian ruler who had endured for more years than the vast majority of his citizens could remember. But he was not so widely perceived as a western lackey as other Arab leaders, accused of putting outside interests before the interests of their people. As the uprising spread and the seriousness of the threat to his rule became apparent, Gaddafi showed he had lost none of the ruthlessness directed against dissidents and exiles in the 1970s and 1980s. Libya had spent 40 years under Gaddafi's uninterrupted rule. With his death, it has virtually ceased to exist. One can hardly regard as fully capable a country where most decisions are made at gunpoint, where there are three governments and two parliaments constantly at odds with each other, where prime ministers take turns in an endless succession, where lawmakers feel free to vote to prolong their own powers, where rich oilfields and ports change hands now and then between rival factions and where many regions are left entirely at the mercy of local warlords. Gaddafi, though cursed by some as a tyrant who mercilessly quashed dissent, outlawed political life, and nipped the opposition in the bud, managed to achieve his prime objective. He built a Libya that was a centralized state and not a territory of warring tribes and clans. His citizens enjoyed rights, fringe benefits, and decent living conditions. Oil revenues were distributed among the Libyans, who enjoyed free education, including an opportunity to receive instruction in other countries, free medical care and social insurance, and could obtain real estate and other properties free of charge or for a token payment. Without such a strong leader the "revolutionary wave" brought to the surface an endless wave of rival Islamic groups many of which promptly turned radical. Many of these associated themselves with Al-Qaeda from the outset. Their militants first fought against Gaddafi and then eagerly joined the Islamic State (outlawed in Russia), which promptly started to thrive in an oil-rich and feud-ravaged country possessing vast military arsenals.

Final Day of Dictatorship

The 1988 bombing of a Pan Am passenger airplane over Lockerbie, Scotland, was blamed on Libyan terrorists, which led to international sanctions on Libya throughout the 1990s. Libya took responsibility for the bombings in 2003, easing the sanctions and leading to better relations with the West. Throughout all, Muammar Gaddafi remained firmly in power and built a reputation as a shrewd, if eccentric, dictator. In 2011, he attacked protesters in his own country, leading to a full-armed rebellion in Libya. An allied group of Arab and Western countries supported the rebellion by attacking Libyan air defenses and establishing a "no-fly zone" over Libya. The rebel forces overran Tripoli in August of 2011. Gaddafi escaped. Gaddafi met his ignominious and grisly end when NTC forces found him hiding in a tunnel following a NATO airstrike on his convoy as he tried to take a break from his last stronghold, the city of Sirte, where it had all begun, But two months later he was wounded in battle after being cornered near his hometown of Sirte; he reportedly was captured and then died of his wounds. The exact circumstances of his death remain in dispute, either "killed in the crossfire", summarily executed, or lynched and dragged through the streets by jubilant, battle-hardened fighters. Though it meant the Libyan people and other victims around the world were robbed of proper justice, the news sparked wild celebrations across his former domain that nearly 42 years of rule and misrule had truly come to a close.

When the policies are away from people then it cannot make the country healthy and wealthy

5) Make policy centralizing people

CHAPTER SEVEN

The Five Finger

As the world struggles to cope with the 2020 pandemic, which first emerged in China, Chinese President Xi Jinping is pursuing his quest for regional dominance more aggressively than ever.

Why Xi Jinping? Why Dominance? Why China?

The Tibetan Palm

The deadly clashes at Galwan and the ongoing standoff between India and China on the ridges or "fingers" around the Pangong Tso are a metaphor for the wider conflict between the two countries. The metaphor refers to all the areas that Chinese strategy refers to as the "five fingers of the Tibetan palm". Mao declared Tibet to be the palm of China whereas Ladakh, Nepal, Sikkim, Bhutan, and North East Frontier Association (NEFA, modern Indian province of Arunachal Pradesh) are its five fingers and it is China's responsibility to 'liberate' them all. Nehru, out of laziness and myopia, still believed that China had no reason to be hostile toward India, even when China 'liberated' Tibet oppressively. Nehru was among the first in the United Nations to recognize the People's Republic of China in 1950 while China never officially recognized the accession of Sikkim to India in 1975. Though Nehru was not alive to realize his callousness in the UN, he got a harder blow of betrayal from his Chinese counterpart, during his lifetime, in 1962 in the form of the Sino-Indian war. The first offensive launched by China was across the MacMahon Line (the international boundary between India and China to the south of Tibet) into the Tawang frontiers of NEFA and across the remnants of the Johnson Line (the international boundary between India and China to the north of Tibet) through Rezang Pass of Ladakh. Ladakh and NEFA were the two 'fingers' who permanently identified themselves as Indian, and China was desperate to annex them. Despite huge resistance, the Indian troops fought an unprepared battle. The People's Liberation Army (PLA) of China managed to advance and grab tracts of lands in AksaiChin, which essentially remained Indian territories till then. There were attempts to establish a treaty after both sides incurred considerable loss to human lives and the exchequer. But things started deteriorating again when Nehru rejected Chinese counterpart Zhou Enlai's claims on MacMahon Line. The diplomatic failure on Nehru's part was again, neither strong support from the US and UK nor the weakest backing from the USSR. An ancient Chinese proverb says, if the Eastern wind does not prevail over the Western wind, then the Eastern wind will prevail over the Eastern wind. Perhaps it was the other Eastern Wind that helped Ladakh and Arunachal-NEFA to remain in their natural Indian habitat.

Dalai Lama

In 1949, seeing that the Communists were gaining control of China, the Kashag expelled all Chinese connected with the Chinese government, over the protests of both the Kuomintang and the Communists. Both the Republic of China (ROC) and the People's Republic of China (PRC) have maintained China's claim to sovereignty over Tibet. Many people felt that Tibet should not be part of China because they were constantly under attack in different ways rather often.The Communist Chinese invasion in 1950 led to years of turmoil, that culminated in the complete overthrow of the Tibetan Government and the self-imposed exile of the Dalai Lama and 100,000 Tibetans in 1959.

His Holiness the 14th Dalai Lama, Tenzin Gyatso, the spiritual leader of Tibet. Tibetan Government and the self-imposed exile of the Dalai Lama and 100,000 Tibetans in 1959. After the invasion of Tibet by the Chinese government, His Holiness was forced to escape into exile. Since then he has been living in Dharamsala, northern India. So then India helped Tibet by saving their leader Dalai Lama.

The Needed Five

According to the construct, attributed to Mao and cited in the 1950s by Chinese officials, Xizang (Tibet) was China's right palm, and it was its responsibility to "liberate" the fingers. Fiver fingers are defined as Ladakh, Nepal, Sikkim, Bhutan, and the North-East Frontier Agency (NEFA, or Arunachal Pradesh). Sixty years ago, India began to set about ensuring that quite the reverse ensued, and all five fingers were more closely attached to India, not China. The little 'finger' Sikkim, though retained its autonomous status for a long since 1947 after the British left, the most popular King Tashi Namgyal of the sacred Chogyal dynasty signed a suzerainty pact with India in 1950. After Tashi, the next Chogyal lost popularity fast enough to pave way for a progressive Kazi Lhendup Dorjee to form Sikkim National Congress. Kazi realized the need to join India on ideological grounds. Sikkimese citizens could never have any appetite toward China for its demonic atrocities in Tibet, the root of Sikkim. In 1975, Sikkim joined the Indian confederation as Kazi's party won a unanimous poll.

Bhutan's long cultural relations of Buddhism with India date back to the 9th century through the migrating Vajrayana Tibetan monks. Though India inherited the British suzerainty on Bhutan post-1947, it gradually moved toward being a partner of Bhutan from a big brother. 2007 Indo-Bhutan treaty is seen as strong Indian patronage toward Bhutan's move toward democracy. Bhutan maintains its watertight Tibetan Buddhist identity and hence feels much safe with India than with China.

It is difficult for the Chinese dragon to digest the truth that though they have forcibly ascended Tibet by all inhuman means, the Exiled Government of Tibet, headed by the Dalai Lama is hosted in the Himalayan city of Dharmasala by India. And the dragon scratched but could never poach in any of the five fingers of Tibet. And hence, China keeps up its attempt to scratch, even now.

India's three-pronged foreign policy

India's defeat in the 1962 war has been studied in great detail, what is perhaps not so well understood is the three-pronged foreign policy New Delhi set into motion at the time, which provided an effective counter to Mao's five-finger policy for the century.

Since 2009, Indian border tracts of Ladakh and Arunachal have been experiencing regular audacious intrusions of Chinese red-caps. They have engineered a Maoist uprising with prolonged bloodshed in Nepal, resulting in an overturn of the pro-India Hindu monarchy. They have constructed mega-dams over the Tsang Po River that flows through the Arunachal and Assam provinces of India, renamed the Brahmaputra, forming their lifeline. The Chinese have laid out highways along the borders, to the rim, for easy and timely transportation of military masses. The object on international forums when premiers of India or the Exiled Government of Tibet visit Arunachal.

India's government under Manmohan Singh is sleeping on these phenomena in the same way Nehru did. India is not responding, even diplomatically and adequately, fearing a second Sino-Indian war that would be retrogressive to India's economic dream run. Well, the same fear could not avoid in the first one and might not escape another in near future. But will history repeat itself? Can the five fingers be protected from being severed? Or, can India ever think of the true liberation of mainland Tibet? Will the Eastern Wind of peace and democracy prevail over the Eastern Wind of ambitions?

The Right Turn

The impact of the new map of Jammu and Kashmir on ties with Nepal as well is no coincidence. There is proof enough that now more than ever, as the government readies its hand on dealing with China, it must not lose sight of every finger in play. But the main man should understand the fingers has their own interest of future planning which each sate working on it.

It reminds us to create a policy that can protect the country from foreign invaders and also not to threat any other country via policy-making in their interest and security. It may also counteract in return.

When our country policy of security is made it is cleared that the next and neiboring country also produce the same.

6) The next country also create policy on security to protect

CHAPTER EIGHT

The Demand for New Constitution

"In a countrywide movement, protesters battle the military-backed government seeking fresh elections, a new Constitution that protects their rights, and radical reform of the monarchy. The 2020 student protests in Thailand are about breaking up the military-monarchy alliance that has prevailed for most of the past 60 years."

Why Thailand? Why such protest? Why Monarchy?

The Young Voices

The protestors are students and young people, and there is no overall leader. Key groups include the Free Youth Movement, which was behind the first major protest, and the United Front of Thammasat and Demonstration, a student group from Bangkok's Thammasat University, which has championed calls for monarchy reform. Then there is the Bad Student movement of high schoolers, which also seeks education reform. Protestors are about ridding the 12-Values propaganda from the education system and ensuring checks and balances on the monarchy in the political system, which has been used as a tool of legitimacy and a legal bludgeon to mute opponents via the draconian lèse majesté law. Ultimately, the protests are about who gets to define and control Thai nationalism. The colloquial use of the term nationalism generally carries a negative connotation, focusing on exclusivity and identity politics. This usage ignores the core idea of nationalism that fueled revolutions across the world in the 19th century, from France to the Americas: that the state belongs to the people. The protesters in Thailand are demanding popular sovereignty. And their savvy use of social media in the 21st-century equivalent of the French Revolution's barricades. The youth-led uprising became widely known for its iconic three-finger salute displayed by tens of thousands in the streets demanding a new democratic constitution be introduced with reforms to the monarchy. The momentum of the protests was seriously disrupted by the pandemic and subsequent lockdown measures, as well as criminal prosecution, violent crackdowns, and harassment of protesters.

The front line of increasingly violent confrontations was in Bangkok's Din Daeng district. Protesters vandalized and burned traffic police booths, police vehicles, and royal portraits. Riot police used water cannons mixed with dye and teargas chemicals, as well as teargas grenades and rubber bullets to disperse the crowds. While the authorities claimed to follow international standards for crowd control, in practice riot police routinely used excessive force against protesters, in some cases causing serious injuries.

The Monarchy

King Maha Vajiralongkorn, also known as Rama X, is the 10th monarch in the Chakri dynasty, which dates back to 1782. He was a student at The King's School in Parramatta and at Duntroon, the Australian Army's officer training college, from 1972 until 1975. Married four times and with seven children, Vajiralongkorn's reputation as a playboy dates back to when he was a young man. Vajiralongkorn is still a bit of an absentee monarch, living mostly in Europe. But that doesn't mean he's detached from politics back home. He has clearly taken charge, doing so in a way that implicitly affirms both obedience to authority and a kind of above-the-law monarchical privilege.

The Criminal Code

Article 112 of the country's criminal code says anyone who "defames, insults or threatens the king, the queen, the heir-apparent or the regent" can be punished with a jail term of between three and 15 years. The law has been used to quell almost all criticism of the royal family. Most of the protest leaders were arrested under this law.

While the protesters' demand for monarchy reform and the removal of Section 112 is not new, tensions over the use of the law have been rising following a string of arrests and charges against student protesters. According to Thai Lawyers for Human Rights, at least 145 people are currently facing charges under Section 112. Local media reported that five activists remain in custody pending trial on royal defamation charges, including protest leaders Parit "Penguin" Chiwarak and human rights lawyer Arnon Nampa. Fellow student activist Patsaravalee "Mind" Tanakitvibulpon, 26, who is out on bail after being accused of lese majeste for a speech she made earlier this year, told ST: "I feel even more determined to fight. Because both the government and the judiciary at this time are unable to give justice to the people."

The Demand

On August 10, the protesters made 10 demands for reforming the monarchy. These included the abolition of the lese-majeste law, cuts to the king's budget, a clear delineation between crown property and the king's personal wealth, and a requirement for the king to be accountable to Parliament as stipulated in the post-revolution constitution of 1932. No such requirement exists under the latest constitution, and royal decrees circumvent Parliament.

The Protest Symbols

The 3 finger salute, now adopted by Thai protesters as their "go-to" symbol in the current round of rallies and protests against the Thai government and establishment, emerged originally from pop culture. Young activists in Thailand have regularly used humor and creativity, said Tracy Beattie, a researcher at the Australian Strategic Policy Institute who specializes in Thai politics. Yellow inflatable rubber ducks have become a new symbol for the pro-democracy movement, not just because they are cute but also because they highlight the sheer absurdity and disproportionality of the situation.

The prime factor of national policy-making should be people and in the wrong way, it can create demand for making a new one.

7) The Prime Factors in making a National Policy are always the Citizens of a country

CHAPTER NINE

The Rised Inflation

"While Sri Lanka's economic difficulties continue to worsen, its food prices are soaring, and its coffers are running empty, the nation looks to be on the verge of a "humanitarian crisis," according to the United Nations Development Programme."

Why such a crisis? Why Sri Lanka?

Reason

For a nation largely reliant on imports of energy supplies, food grains, essential commodities, and medications, having a foreign reserve of just $2.31 billion is a financial nightmare for the government. The admission by President Gotabaya Rajapaksa that his nation is running a trade imbalance of $10 billion does nothing to alleviate the issue in the least. In his position as an experienced politician who was regarded as a significant strategist in Colombo's struggle against the LTTE about a decade and a half ago, he and his brothers should have been well aware of the legacy they were receiving from their forefathers. The tax reduction bonanza implemented in 2019 did not provide the intended effects, resulting in a revenue loss.

Mismanagement by Successive Governments

On the surface, the cause for Sri Lanka's current economic crisis can be attributed to economic mismanagement by successive governments and a string of ill-advised decisions such as banning the use of chemical fertilizers and deep tax cuts promised by President Rajapaksha during his 2019 election campaign months before the 2021 pandemic decimated Sri Lanka's major tourism sector and also stopped foreign remittances. The economic crisis began a little over two years ago and during that time Sri Lanka has exhausted over 70% of its foreign reserves and now is only left with $2 billion in foreign reserves. In addition, Sri Lanka also has a whopping $7 billion in debt due in 2022. And that is where the main problem lies, Sri Lanka's ever-growing debt and its overreliance on China for money for investments in infrastructure projects for the island nation.

With Red Flag

In the early 2000s, Sri Lanka adopted an infrastructure-centric growth model based on China's growth model hoping that it would be able to create jobs and usher prosperity for the island nation. And Sri Lanka turned to China for money to fund its infrastructure projects. As per reports, China has invested $12 billion in Sri Lanka's infrastructure projects from 2006 to 2019 and continues to fund infrastructure projects like the Colombo Port City which is being built by a Chinese state-owned enterprise called China Communications Construction Company at the cost of $1.4 billion. The project is expected to complete in 2043, meaning Sri Lanka is unlikely to get any revenue from the project for close to two decades. Even after completion, 43% of the reclaimed land will be leased to China for 99 years because Sri Lanka has no other way to finance it. Essentially, Sri Lanka has been caught in a vicious cycle of lending money from China for infrastructure projects and being unable to pay them back, resulting in Sri Lanka having to either give up control of the projects or take out other loans to pay China back. The most infamous case is that of the port of Hambantota. In the early 2010s, Sri Lanka's former President Mahinda Rajapaksa wanted to build a port in his home region of Hambantota, but requests for funds were rejected numerous times by multiple entities due to the port not having commercial viability. China's investments in Sri Lanka date back to the 1970s. During then China used to provide Sri Lanka with outright grants and in the 2000s that relationship has 'upgraded' to a commercial model that utilized interest-bearing loans and infrastructure-related foreign direct investment. During the administration of President Mahinda Rajapaksa China invested in key infrastructure projects in Sri Lanka such as transport, energy, and telecommunications project.

High Inflation

Sri Lanka is currently in the worst economic crisis since the country's founding. High inflation rates have made it harder for Sri Lankans to buy daily necessities, the country has been experiencing 13-hour-long power cuts and people have to stand in line for hours for fuel. With the country's foreign reserves dwindling there are fears that the country will not be able to repay its foreign debt. A lot of its current problems can be attributed to short term blunders by the Sri Lankan government but a deep study of the country's economic history will reveal China's heavy investment and its influence in pushing Sri Lanka to take on more debt to build non-economically viable infrastructure projects has led it here. Between 2012-and 2016 China accounted for 30% of all Foreign Direct Investment into Sri Lanka. Chinese loans and equity are funding an estimated 50 major and minor projects in Sri Lanka worth $11 billion. Not only large-scale projects like Hambantota Port and Colombo Port City but also roads and water treatment plants. Chinese loans also come at a much higher interest rate (6.5% per annum) than those from the Asian Development Bank (2.5%-3% per annum). In 2017, the Sri Lankan government spent 83% of its revenue on debt repayment. Looking at these bleak statistics, it is no wonder that the Sri Lankan government choose to convert its debt into equity and hand over Hambantota port to China. Sri Lanka's crushing external debt is one of the main causes of its current economic crisis and has forced the country to repeatedly devalue its currency just to be able to buy food for its people.

To work on five different areas

The threat of Chinese Influence: With such an economic situation and with the fact that the Sri Lankan government has asked for a 2.5 Bn USD emergency aid from China, there is a threat that China may gain influence in the island country. It is trying a lot for the last few years but owing to Indian diplomacy, things could not succeed the way the dragon wanted currently things are different now. Since the location of Sri Lanka is strategic, India must be cautious of every Chinese attempt to influence Sri Lanka.

Economic Aspects: Although India does not have many imports from Sri Lanka and less than 1 Bn USD worth of goods are imported, there is a serious economic threat in terms of handling Indian Trans-Shipments. Sri Lanka is an important Trans-Shipment hub that handles nearly 48% of our International Cargo. Today due to the absence of labor, non-availability of vehicles to transport our containers between ports, and the closing down of port facilities, a large number of Indian shipments are lying at Sri Lankan

Ports. It is not the only thing, nearly 22% of total Sri Lanka's GDP comes from factors lined to India. These are trade, tourism & remittances. These factors will certainly get affected by the present situation in Sri Lanka.

Refugee Crisis: India witnessed that whenever there is a political or social crisis in Sri Lanka, a large number of refugees come from the Sinhala Land to India through the Palk strait & Gulf of Munnar. The first reason is that the people belong to the same Tamil Community and are connected for centuries and the second is that after the Sri Lankan Civil war, the faith of the ethnic Tamil community has been reduced in the Sri Lankan government. India may find it difficult to handle such a big influx of refugees. We witnessed it in the nineties but this time it is going to be more severe. A large number of refugees have already started coming and India needs to form a strong policy to handle this issue.

Rise of Rebel Groups in Sri Lanka: Although Sri Lanka claimed that it eliminated Tamil Rebel groups by 2009, things are still boiling inside. Tamils have not yet gotten a proper representation in the government they are ignored most in these times. This economic crisis may give a new life to already redundant rebels who are trying to find a cause to fuel up the issue. Not only Tamil Rebels but there are several dissident groups among the ethnic Sinhalese population too and we can not rule out the possibility of them picking weapons in this time of crisis.

Humanitarian Crisis: India is the only immediate neighbor of Sri Lanka and as we see, there is a bigger threat of a large-scale humanitarian crisis looming over the country. There is no food, there are no medicines, there is no law & order too and in case of a big crisis like civil war or any other humanitarian crisis, the entire onus will lie on India to help. India will be a via media to transfer International Aid too and this will put additional pressure on our economy. This will have positive as well as negative impacts too.

Policy-making in a crisis is different from routine, It needs next thinking on handling different areas, and also handling it instant, continuous, and progressive. The coming policy-making should exercise policy on taking all the areas mentioned above to solve the crisis

8) Policy-making in crisis needs a mind of unifying diverse areas

CHAPTER TEN

The Red Flag of Avenge

The Red Flag of Avenge

The United States and Iran are once again on the verge of conflict. Iran responded to the Soleimani assassination by launching a volley of missiles at a United States military base. United States sanctions have severely damaged the Iranian economy, GDP shrunk by 9.5 percent, inflation is near 40 percent, and oil exports have fallen by 80 percent. So the baseline of the conflict sparked out.

Why Iran and US? Who is Soleimani? Why the red flag notice?

The Branch

The decades-old feud between them is exacerbated by religious differences. They each follow one of the two main branches of Islam. Iran is largely Shia Muslim, while Saudi Arabia sees itself as the leading Sunni Muslim power. Also Saudi Ties with United States where very close for years. Successive U.S. Administrations have referred to the Saudi government as an important partner, and U.S. arms sales and related security cooperation have continued with congressional oversight and some congressional opposition.

The New Rise

The region of West Asia/Middle East has borne witness to the emerging power of Iran, which has in certain cases through the exploitation of the tumult of the Arab Spring, spread its far-reaching tentacles to Syria and Yemen. The drastic shift in the power dynamic in the region has resulted in Iran emerging as a leading influential player to occupy the dominant seat in deciding how the regional affairs are being shaped. Which cannot be bared by capitalistic country due to oil wealth of Iran. President Clinton in March 1995 issued Executive Order 12957 to prohibit US trade in Iran's oil industry, and in May 1995 issued Executive Order 12959 to prohibit all US trade with Iran. Trade with the United States, which had been growing since the end of the Iran Iraq War, ended abruptly.

The Sanctions

The US move on Prohibition of all US trade(Sanctions) with Iran made a huge fall on Iran economic stand. United States sanctions have severely damaged the Iranian economy, GDP shrunk by 9.5 percent, inflation is near 40 percent, and oil exports have fallen by 80 percent. The Iran government dominated the Persian gulf and Gulf of Oman to respond the sanctions and also seized ships of US friendly countries that build the tension to US and US allied nations. British Royal Marines helped seize Iranian tanker Grace 1 near Gibraltar which was suspected of breaking EU sanctions, infuriating Iran. Iran's foreign minister Javad Zarif said in a tweet the UK "must cease being an accessory to #Economic Terrorism of the US".

The Tale of Capitalist Reaction

Three American drones moved into position overhead, with no fear of challenge in an Iraqi airspace completely dominated by the U.S. military. Each was armed with four Hellfire missiles. On large screens, various U.S. officials watched as an Iraqi militia leader walked up a set of stairs to greet the leader of Iran's Quds Force as he emerged from the airplane. The men on the ground had no idea that their lives were now to be measured in minutes. The drones followed as the vehicles began moving to exit the airport. Those watching could see the missiles strike, a man made bolt from the sky. The vehicles were engulfed in a fireball. In total, four missiles were fired. There were no survivors. Soleimani, who had helped kill Americans for more than a decade, was no more. Top Iranian general

Qasem Soleimani assassinated by US Baghdad air strike.

The Red Flag

The assassination of Qassem Soleimani has been an unexpected bounty for the Islamic Republic at a time when Iran was balancing multiple economic, domestic and regional pressures stemming from the Trump administration's maximum pressure campaign. Iran supreme leader Ayatollah Ali Khamenei appeared to cry as he prayed over the flag-draped coffins containing the remains of Soleimani. The massive funeral scenes in multiple Iranian cities displaying unending waves of mourners chanting against the United States has provided the Islamic Republic with a unique opportunity to showcase its mobilizing potential. Iran hoisted a symbolic red flag atop a mosque in the Shiite holy city of Qom following the killing of its commander Qassim Suleimani. The flag hoisting ceremony further underlines the seriousness of Iran's call for avenging the death of the head of its elite Quds force.

The action on destroying can make the supporting factors to eye on rest days

9) Action on destroying policies cannot bring up peace

CHAPTER ELEVEN

The Friendship and Threats

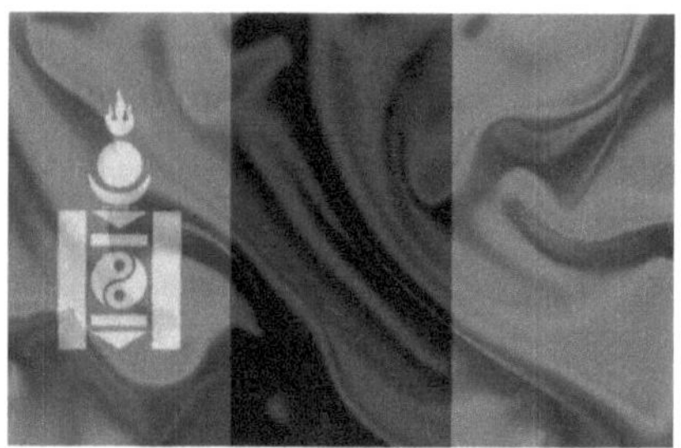

While being sandwiched between China and Russia, Mongolia has been trying to build relations with its third neighbors the US, South Korea, Japan and European countries to balance the influence of its physical neighbors China and Russia. The heart of Mongolia's third neighbor foreign policy is to ensure relations with its two neighbors while encouraging other countries that are developed and wealthy to take interest in Mongolia's development.

Why Mongolia? Why third neighbor? Why Threats?

Mongolia

Landlocked Mongolia is located between Russia to the north and China to the south, deep within the interior of eastern Asia far from any ocean. The country has a marked continental climate, with long cold winters and short cool-to-hot summers. Its remarkable variety of scenery consists largely of upland steppes, semideserts, and deserts, although in the west and north forested high mountain ranges alternate with lake-dotted basins. Mongol leader Genghis Khan (1162-1227) rose from humble beginnings to establish the largest land empire in history.

The Mongol History with Genghis Khan

Before Genghis Khan became the leader of Mongolia, he was known as Temujin. He was born around 1162 in modern-day northern Mongolia into a nomadic tribe with noble ties and powerful alliances. These fortunate circumstances helped him unite dozens of tribes in his adulthood via alliances. War ensued, and Temujin prevailed, destroying all the remaining rival tribes from 1203–1205 and bringing them under his sway. In 1206, Temujin was crowned as the leader of the Great Mongol Nation. It was then that he assumed the title of Genghis Khan, meaning universal leader, marking the start of the Mongol Empire. Genghis Khan ruled between 1206 and 1227, expanding trade across Asia and into eastern Europe, enacting relatively tolerant social and religious laws, and leading devastating military campaigns that left local populations depleted and fearful of the brutal Mongol forces. He also utilized a lenient policy toward religious and local traditions, which convinced many people to follow his lead with promises of amnesty and neutrality.

The Handshakes

Battulga,The President is largely seen as a pro-Russian politician due to his Russian ties and his knowledge of the Russian language. He is commonly compared to Russian President Vladimir Putin due to their shared love and experience in judo. Today its economy is so dependent on China that it risks becoming a client state once again. But also China-Mongolia cooperation on COVID-19 shows deep friendship. It depends upon the China's expansion and threats in coming days.

The Third

It would be hard to find a country that has more at stake in the outcome of U.S. China strategic competition than Mongolia or that better demonstrates why that competition is not a lost cause. With only some 3 million citizens occupying a large territory rich in natural resources sharing a long land border with under-resourced China's population of 1.4 billion, Mongolia's security situation is "intense," in the words of the commander of its armed forces. But Mongolians will not bend to Chinese domination.

The Visit

Ironically when one thinks of Mongolia the utter winter, cold climate, distance and exotic nature claim the mind space. But this is one country where India and the Indians are simply loved. Perhaps, due to the Buddhist connection and Himalayan heritage of the Mongolian people. India and Mongolia embarked on a journey of ever enhancing cooperation and becoming strategic partners during 2015 visit of Prime Minister Narendra Modi. He had announced a one billion dollar line of credit for the development of infrastructure in Mongolia and so on. The two countries along with Bhutan had moved UN for the recognition of Bangladesh and hence the political synergy is quite clearly evident and can be further built upon for the mutual benefit.

The New Education Curriculum of China

Ethnic Mongolian students and parents in northern China have staged mass school boycotts over a new curriculum that would scale back education in their mother tongue, in a rare and highly visible protest against the ruling Communist Party's intensified push for ethnic assimilation. Under the new policy, Mandarin Chinese will replace Mongolian as the medium of instruction for three subjects in elementary and middle schools for minority groups across the Inner Mongolia Autonomous Region. The start is in the own country of China but it may lead to Mongolia with cultural bond of Autonomous region of China and Mongolia. But the threat of friendship, Mongols have already learnt from their historical leader how to deal it.

- 10) It's good to find and stay in the made policies until it turns

CHAPTER TWELVE

The Socialist Republic

The Socialist Republic

During the Vietnam war, more than 47,000 American soldiers were killed, while Vietnam saw more than two million casualties of troops and civilians from both the partitioned North and South Vietnam. But Vietnam is now regarded as America's closest ally in Southeast Asia with Communist policies in State.Vietnam's consistent policy of enhancing the solidarity, friendship and comprehensive strategic cooperation with Russia, which is also the top priority in the foreign policy of the Vietnamese

(Communist) Party, state and army.

Why Vietnam? What kind of war? Is it a Change to capitalist communists ?

Vietnam war?

The Vietnam War was a long, costly and divisive conflict that pitted the communist government of North Vietnam against South Vietnam and its principal ally, the United States. The conflict was intensified by the ongoing Cold War between the United States and the Soviet Union. More than 3 million people including over 58,000 Americans were killed in the Vietnam War, and more than half of the dead were Vietnamese civilians. Opposition to the war in the United States bitterly divided Americans, even after President Richard Nixon ordered the withdrawal of U.S. forces in 1973. Communist forces ended the war by seizing control of South Vietnam in 1975, and the country was unified as the Socialist Republic of Vietnam.

The Unification

The above paragraph consists of two Vietnam north and south, But it said to be as one now, because of the unification in 1976. While the Paris agreement brought an end to years of bitter warfare between the United States and North Vietnam, it did not bring peace to South Vietnam. By March 1975, two years and two months after the signing of the Paris peace agreement, the South Vietnamese Army was in full retreat before a superior communist force. A year later, on July 2, 1976, North and South Vietnam were finally unified. Saigon became Ho Chi Minh City, and Hanoi became the capital of the new

Socialist Republic of Vietnam.

The American Relationship

Since the normalization of bilateral relations in 1995, U.S.-Vietnam relations have become increasingly cooperative and comprehensive, evolving into a flourishing partnership that spans political, economic, security, and people-to-people ties. The United States supports a strong, prosperous, and independent Vietnam that contributes to international security; engages in fair and reciprocal trade; and respects human rights and the rule of law.

The Asian Relationship

Russia was one of the first countries to establish diplomatic relations with Vietnam, laying the groundwork for a strong bilateral and economic relationship between the countries. Vietnam and Russia set up a strategic partnership back in 2001 and elevated this relationship to a comprehensive strategic partnership in 2012 paving the way for increasing economic ties. Major Russian oil and gas groups like Gazprom and Rosneft are expected to engage in many more projects in Vietnam's continental shelf by 2030.

It take a effort to build a diplomatic relationship with world Largest political powers. On making the nation as a good socialistic country with the policies of the largest democracies.

The Covid Pull

China's actions in the South China Sea and along the Line of Actual Control (LAC) figured in the discussions, with both sides briefing each other on the latest developments, India and Vietnam agreed to enhance bilateral cooperation in line with Indo-Pacific Oceans Initiative and Asean's outlook on Indo-Pacific to "achieve shared security, prosperity and growth for all in the region", In recent years, Vietnam has often turned to India for support over China's increasing activities within its exclusive economic zone in the South China Sea.

The Turn

The Hope may be elevated due to the cooperation of the Vietnam government towards the illegal steps in South China sea. More than holding the policies to turn capitalism or communism the concept of socialism wins to bring security and peace.

- 11) Create an option of fusion when it is progressive

CHAPTER THIRTEEN

The Lost Unity

"As World War II dragged to an end in 1945, the leaders of the "Big Three" allied powers the United States, Soviet Union, and Great Britain met in Potsdam, Germany, to hash out terms to conclude the bloodiest conflict the world had ever seen. The great powers split Germany into occupation zones, recognized a Soviet-backed government in Poland, and partitioned Vietnam, monumental decisions that shaped the postwar global order. The talks were meant to forge a lasting peace, but within 18 months, a Cold War began that lasted more decades."

Why Three Powers? Why such cold war?

The History of Integeration

On December 28, 1922, the Treaty of Creation of the USSR was approved during a conference of plenipotentiary delegations from the Russian SFSR, the Transcaucasian SFSR, the Ukrainian SSR, and the Byelorussian SSR. The announcement was made at the stage of the Bolshoi Theatre. On February 1, 1924, the United Kingdom recognised the USSR as a country. The constitution of the USSR was approved in December 1922. On April 3, 1922, Stalin, the General Secretary of the Communist Party of the Soviet Union, was appointed. Lenin had appointed Stalin the head of the Workers' and Peasants' Inspectorate, which gave Stalin considerable power. In 1928, Stalin introduced the first five-year plan for building a socialist economy. The five-year plans were designed following the communist ideology and giving an equal share to everyone in the economy. In September 1934, the country joined the League of Nations, which was the first worldwide intergovernmental organisation set up to maintain world peace. On December 14, 1939, the Soviet Union was expelled from League of Nations for invading Finland.

The Policy

In the late 1980s, the government appeared to have many characteristics in common with liberal democratic political systems. For instance, a constitution established all organizations of government and granted to citizens a series of political and civic rights. A legislative body, the Congress of People's Deputies, and its standing legislature, the Supreme Soviet, represented the principle of popular sovereignty. The Supreme Soviet, which had an elected chairman who functioned as head of state, oversaw the Council of Ministers, which acted as the executive branch of the government. The chairman of the Council of Ministers, whose selection was approved by the legislative branch, functioned as head of government. A constitutionally based judicial branch of government included a court system, headed by the Supreme Court, that was responsible for overseeing the observance of Soviet law by government bodies. According to the 1977 Soviet Constitution, the government had a federal structure, permitting the republics some authority over policy implementation and offering the national minorities the appearance of participation in the management of their own affairs.

In practice, however, the government differed markedly from Western systems. In the late 1980s, the CPSU performed many functions that governments of other countries usually perform. For example, the party decided on the policy alternatives that the government ultimately implemented. The government merely ratified the party's decisions to lend them an aura of legitimacy. The CPSU used a variety of mechanisms to ensure that the government adhered to its policies. The party, using its nomenklatura authority, placed its loyalists in leadership positions throughout the government, where they were subject to the norms of democratic centralism. Party bodies closely monitored the actions of government ministries, agencies, and legislative organs.

The content of the Soviet Constitution differed in many ways from typical Western constitutions. It generally described existing political relationships, as determined by the CPSU, rather than prescribing an ideal set of political relationships. The Constitution was long and detailed, giving technical specifications for individual organs of government. The Constitution included political statements, such as foreign policy goals, and provided a theoretical definition of the state within the ideological framework of Marxism-Leninism. The CPSU leadership could radically change the constitution or remake it completely, as it did several times throughout its history.

The Council of Ministers acted as the executive body of the government. Its most important duties lay in the administration of the economy. The council was thoroughly under the control of the CPSU, and its chairman - the Soviet prime minister was always a member of the Politburo. The council, which in 1989 included more than 100 members, was too large and unwieldy to act as a unified executive body. The council's Presidium, made up of the leading economic administrators and led by the chairman, exercised dominant power within the Council of Ministers.

According to the Constitution, as amended in 1988, the highest legislative body in the Soviet Union was the Congress of People's Deputies, which convened for the first time in May 1989. The main tasks of the congress were the election of the standing legislature, the Supreme Soviet, and the election of the chairman of the Supreme Soviet, who acted as head of state. Theoretically, the Congress of People's Deputies and the Supreme Soviet wielded enormous legislative power. In practice, however, the Congress of People's Deputies met infrequently and only to approve decisions made by the party, the Council of Ministers, and its own Supreme Soviet. The Supreme Soviet, the Presidium of the Supreme Soviet, the chairman of the Supreme Soviet, and the Council of Ministers had substantial authority to enact laws, decrees, resolutions, and orders binding on the population. The Congress of

People's Deputies had the authority to ratify these decisions.

The judiciary was not independent. The Supreme Court supervised the lower courts and applied the law as established by the Constitution or as interpreted by the Supreme Soviet. The Constitutional Oversight Committee reviewed the constitutionality of laws and acts. The Soviet Union lacked an adversarial court procedure known to common law jurisdictions. Rather, Soviet law utilised the system derived from Roman law, where judge, procurator and defense attorney worked collaboratively to establish the truth.

The Soviet Union was a federal state made up of fifteen republics joined together in a theoretically voluntary union. In turn, a series of territorial units made up the republics. The republics also contained jurisdictions intended to protect the interests of national minorities. The republics had their own constitutions, which, along with the all union Constitution, provide the theoretical division of power in the Soviet Union. In 1989, however, the CPSU and the central government retained all significant authority, setting policies that were executed by republic, provincial, oblast, and district governments.

End of Union

In 1990, Latvia and Estonia declared the restoration of their full independence. Gorbachev, who was the general secretary, could not control territories beyond Moscow. By December 1990, all republics had disintegrated from the USSR, while Russia and Kazakhstan didn't. Ukraine, the second-largest republic of the USSR, announced its independence in 1991.

Why Named Sputnik

The name Sputnik is a rocket was an uncrewed orbital carrier rocket designed by Sergei Korolev in the Soviet Union, derived from the R-7 Semyorka ICBM. On 4 October 1957, it was used to perform the world's first satellite launch, placing Sputnik 1 into a low Earth orbit. The Space Race was a 20th-century competition between two Cold War rivals, the Soviet Union (USSR) and the United States (US), to achieve firsts in spaceflight capability. It had its origins in the ballistic missile-based nuclear arms race between the two nations following World War II. The technological advantage required to rapidly achieve spaceflight milestones was seen as necessary for national security, and mixed with the symbolism and ideology of the time. The Space Race led to pioneering efforts to launch artificial satellites, uncrewed space probes of the Moon, Venus, and Mars, and human spaceflight in low Earth orbit and to the Moon. The competition began in earnest on August 2, 1955, when the Soviet Union responded to the US announcement four days earlier of intent to launch artificial satellites for the International Geophysical Year, by declaring they would also launch a satellite "in the near future". The Soviet Union achieved the first successful launch with the October 4, 1957, orbiting of Sputnik 1, and sent the first human to space with the orbital flight of Yuri Gagarin on April 12, 1961

Vaccine of Russia

Russia is open to international cooperation in fighting the global threat of the 2021 pandemic as well as future pandemics. Russia has named its first approved COVID-19 vaccine 'Sputnik V' for the foreign markets. It is a reference to the world's first satellite Sputnik and what Moscow sees as its success at becoming the first country to approve a vaccine. Russia, the largest country on Earth in terms of landmass, is the 11th-largest economy in the world, with a nominal GDP of $1.63 trillion. Russia moves up the ladder to the sixth spot for rankings, with a $4.21 trillion GDP based on PPP. The final conclusion Russia is trying to uphold the lost reputation on economic status with other countries help of the covid vaccine. So as a symbolic representation the Russian Government named the vaccine as Sputnik were it could give the winning of vaccine race, Same as the Space race. But after the Covid war it walked into the Ukrain war.

- 12) One to win and the other to war cannot help peace

CHAPTER FOURTEEN

Endless War

As the crisis over Ukraine escalates, a nascent antiwar movement is demanding that the United States avoid war with Russia. The movement of U.S. troops into Eastern Europe, supplying weapons and equipment to Ukraine, and presidential language opposing Russian actions have inspired some activists. They argue that the situation today is like that in 2003 when the United States began preparations for war against Iraq. But is the United States preparing for a war?

The war in Afghanistan has now dragged on for 17 years,

under Presidents George Bush, Bill Clinton, Barack Obama, Donald Trump and ends with Biden. Obama campaigned on ending the wars in Iraq and Afghanistan, then reneged after his election; and candidate Trump, who deplored the many soldiers being "led to senseless slaughter" in Afghanistan, promptly sent an additional 4,000 troops there after he became president. As interesting and revealing as this discussion at West Point certainly is, it fails to identify the main reason why the United States keeps getting embroiled in so many prolonged wars and military incursions. The only way to find the answer to this question is to pose the ancient Roman question: Qui bono? Who benefits from perpetual warfare?

Although never acknowledged by U.S. political leaders, and seldom by even the U.S. media – is the country's military industrial complex. The big arms manufacturers profit enormously from wars and other armed conflicts. In fact, without continuous and prolonged warfare that requires the deployment of their guns, bombs, tanks, warships and submarines, they would go out of business.

The American military budget is $778 billion in 2020. This massive amount is the second largest item in the country's budget after social security. It is four times more than China's military budget of $216 billion, and 10 times bigger than Russia's budget of just $84.5 billion. In total, the United States spends more on "defense" than the next nine countries combined. It's difficult to find out how much of the colossal U.S. military budget each of them receives. The latest figures I could find (undoubtedly not up to date) were \$36 billion for Lochhead Martin, \$27.6 billion for Boeing, 26.9 billion for BAE Systems, \$22.5 billion for Raytheon, and \$21.6 billion for General Dynamics. But there are dozens of other arms producers that are also awarded contracts. Together, they probably receive and profit from at least half, more likely two-thirds, of that huge \$886 billion war bonanza. These corporations depend on the United States being continually at war against some country somewhere – and now against terrorists everywhere. The weapons of war they produce are made to be used, not stockpiled. If world peace were ever actually to be achieved, they would be bankrupted, unless they could switch to manufacturing things that aren't designed to kill people.

The Ukraine - Russia war defines it direcrtly after the end of Afghanistan war somewhere it kindled to have a war space in the world and Ukraine stuck with the war unfortunate. The number of major wars has also descended from a recent peak. Despite Russian President Vladimir Putin menacing Ukraine, states rarely go to war with one another. More local conflicts rage than ever, but they tend to be of lower intensity. For the most part, 21st-century wars are less lethal than their 20th-century predecessors. Battle deaths, after all, tell just a fraction of the story. Yemen's conflict kills more people, mostly women and young children, due to starvation or preventable disease than violence. Millions of Ethiopians suffer acute food insecurity because of the country's civil war. Fighting involving Islamists elsewhere in Africa often doesn't entail thousands of deaths but drives millions of people from their homes and causes humanitarian devastation. Afghanistan's violence levels have sharply dropped since the Taliban seized power in August, but starvation, caused mostly by Western policies, could leave more Afghans dead including millions of children—than past decades of fighting. Worldwide, the number of displaced people, most due to war, is at a record high. Battle deaths may be down, in other words, but suffering due to conflict is not. Moreover, states compete fiercely even when they're not fighting directly. They do battle with cyberattacks, disinformation campaigns, election interference, economic coercion, and by instrumentalizing migrants. Major and regional powers vie for influence, often through local allies, in war zones. Proxy fighting has not so far sparked direct confrontation among meddling states. Indeed, some navigate the danger adeptly: Russia and Turkey maintain cordial relations despite backing competing sides in the Syrian and Libyan conflicts. Still, foreign involvement in conflicts creates the risk that local clashes light bigger fires.Standoffs involving major powers look increasingly dangerous. Putin may gamble on another incursion into Ukraine. A China-U.S. clash over Taiwan is unlikely in 2022, but the Chinese and U.S. militaries increasingly bump up against each another around the island and in the South China Sea, with all the peril of entanglement that entails. If the Iran nuclear deal collapses, which now seems probable, the United States or Israel may attempt possibly even early in 2022 to knock out Iranian nuclear facilities, likely prompting Tehran to sprint toward weaponization while lashing out across the region. One mishap or miscalculation, in other words, and interstate war could make a comeback. And whatever one thinks of U.S. influence, its decline inevitably brings hazards, given that American might and alliances have structured global affairs for decades. No one should exaggerate the decay: U.S.

forces are still deployed around the globe, NATO stands, and Washington's Asia diplomacy shows it can still marshal coalitions like no other power. But with much in flux, Washington's rivals are probing to see how far they can go.

The Continuous involvement in a war somewhere ignites the reading minds to doubt on military arm resources business on making war could help. But the policy to stay democratic and peace-making rests behind away from the makers.

13) A Policy is on the field not only on papers and thoughts

CHAPTER FIFTEEN

The Rush to India

The Spike on the Ukraine is on between two major blocs. There's the US, along with its allies in the West and the Indo-Pacific, on one side. On the other end are Russia and China. Russia's invasion of Ukraine, and the sharp polarisation that it has led to, are the triggers. India has called for a ceasefire and diplomatic solution to the ongoing crisis. It also refrained from backing a Russian resolution that sought to deflect the blame for the humanitarian crisis it has created in Ukraine. But that's not enough for the West, which has been pressing New Delhi to shift its position at the United Nations, where it has consistently abstained from resolutions criticising Moscow for its actions. Then there is the fact that India continues to buy Russian crude oil, even as pressure mounts to isolate the Kremlin.

The US and Australia condemned India for considering a plan to make rupee- ruble-denominated payments using an alternative to SWIFT. The plan involves making payments using Russia's messaging system, SPFS. The US and its allies fear such arrangements would undermine the sanctions imposed by them.

While India deals with the challenges arising from the Ukraine conflict, it should also look at the emerging opportunities. Relations with Moscow are important because of the defence and strategic ties with India. India has also found strategic convergence with the US, other Quad countries and some western nations when it comes to Chinese aggression. Equally important is the fact that trade volume with Russia is small compared to how much India trades with the US and its allies. These trade ties, take for example Japan's recently announced investments, are vital for India. The government will have to find a way to deftly balance these diverging interests.

There are a number of future scenarios that could unfold, setting forth a new geometry in India's foreign policy. India's response to the Ukraine crisis and the ensuing geopolitical fissures have unfolded a divided debate on the direction of India's foreign policy. Will India, after testing the grounds of engagement with the West come full circle back to a newer version of non-alignment? Despite some hiccups in the tilt to the West, will India, given the mounting China challenge, stick to its commitments to the Quad and its strategic permutations and combinations? Alternatively, will the current geopolitical churning, and louder calls for choosing sides in the international system, lead to a new offspring of understanding in the triangular formation of Russia, India, and China? Ultimately, India's foreign policy direction may not follow any of these geometric designs, but rather take a more flexible path. These formulations may at the outset seem contradictory, but the test of a foreign policy is in holding contrasting directions and still finding the dexterity to operate and move in order to protect and promote India's national interests.

The ultimate view on this is due to the matured foreign policy india have and the world countries found it is also working positive for India. To make a alternative market from China, India can fulfil the policy wise position with the global communication and thats the place where India has been highlighted in the recent days to make high profiled Diplomats and Leaders to visit Delhi

Fingers on Suggestions

A glance on the suggested policy making ideas in the book

CHAPTER SIXTEEN

Policy Making

The book may question you about the link between the incidents, or you may find many links between countries irrespective of the timelines. But the book centralizes people directly and indirectly to find peace. The right policy-making is very important. Do's and don'ts which were scripted in the past pages with the incidents are not complete work of any policy-sixking but to suggest the future policy-makers to note down.

The right policy of stimulating the economy is very important and also it can make a dark history of killing millions when progressed opposite. And "The Great Famine" described the need for it.

Creating the right policy is very important, Finding it right is in hands of makers, increasing the human development index. Glitches in making the right policy can create a dark history

1) Create a Right Policy

Changes in the policy should be futuristic, only then it can find the way to sustainable development. Same when it comes to Finance, A economic policy should be futuristic and progressive, only then it can make the coming days safe.

2) Create a policy futuristic and progressive

The shift in a policy can be made only when the conservative areas are derived, If not, it can make us violate our policies later.

3) A healthy shift in policy should create a wealthy economy

The Delay on good policy is not good when it ignores the economic stimulation, Making a country politically strong and increasing the productivity of making policy is very important when it can stimulate the economy and grow up the country

4) A delay in making the right policy can ignore the economic stimulation

When the policies are away from people then it cannot make the country healthy and wealthy

5) Make policy centralizing people

When our country's policy of security is made, It is clear that the next and neighboring countries also produce the same.

6) The next country also creates policy on security to protect

The prime factor of national policy-making should be people and in the wrong way, it can create demand for making a new one.

7) The Prime Factors in making a National Policy are always the Citizens of a country

Policy-making in a crisis is different from routine, It needs next thinking on handling different areas, and also handling it instant, continuous, and progressive. The coming policy-making should exercise policy on taking all the areas mentioned above to solve the crisis

8) Policy-making in crisis needs a mind of unifying diverse areas

The action on destroying can make the supporting factors to eye on rest days

9) Action on destroying policies cannot bring up peace

10) It's good to find and stay in the made policies until it turns

11) Create an option of fusion when it is progressive

To name the vaccine as Sputnik were it could give the winning of vaccine race, Same as the Space race. But after the Covid war, it walked into the Ukrain war.

12) One to win and the other to war cannot help peace

The Continuous involvement in a war somewhere ignites the reading minds to doubt on military arm resources business on making war could help. But the policy to stay democratic and peace-making rests behind away from the makers.

13) A Policy is on the field not only on papers and thoughts

Sustainable Deveopment Gioals

We are all in a place to work on the SDG which can make this planet glow green. Also, it can bring a better healthy lifestyle for ourselves and our circle. We need co-operation to explore the results of its binding global policies. How we turn ourselves together when it comes to the national interest, we should also wake and make togetherness in global interests in which the pre-planned goals of it can help us to do it.

Sustainable Development Goals

Create Future

Dear Reader,

I'm Glad meeting you via this book, You may come with many incidents such and you may kindled your thought which can be ethical. It may question how these incidents create glitches and are they in numbers? I say "No" to this due to the infinite incidents creating policy glitches. It is our responsibility to learn and continue making the best out of it to make this planet a better place to live. Thank you for choosing my thoughts with one of your great collections. I never know whether it is the one right thing to impact you find errors on this. But it may wake up your idea on the future world if positive human centralized policies coming t o action.

Tranquility wins..!

Thanks,
- Vigneshwaran Ganapathi